12-14-01

Faith,

I hope your memories of Charleston are all good ones.

Good luck in graduate school.

Fondly,
Susan Frawley

The Majesty of
CHARLESTON

Photography and Text by
Peter Beney

PELICAN PUBLISHING COMPANY
Gretna 1993

The word "Pelican" and the depiction of a pelican are trademarks of Pelican
Publishing Company, Inc., and are registered in the U.S. Patent and
Trademark Office.

Library of Congress Cataloging-in-Publication Data

Beney, Peter
    The majesty of Charleston / photography and text by Peter Beney.
      p. cm.
    ISBN 0-88289-955-4
    Charleston (S.C.)—Pictorial works. I. Title.
    F279.C443B46   1993
    975.7'915—dc20   93-10099
                                                        CIP

Photo on p. 2: The City Hall Council Chamber at 80 Broad Street
dates from 1801, and opened as the First Bank of the United States.
In 1818 the City of Charleston purchased it to use as their City Hall.
The Council chamber has many historic paintings, busts, and art
objects on display, and is open to the public. Twice a month the
mayor and council meet here sitting at the original black walnut
desks.

Photo on p. 6: Fountain in Waterfront Park.

Photo on p. 8: Basketwork typical of Charleston.

Book design by Dana Bilbray

Manufactured in Hong Kong
Published by Pelican Publishing Company, Inc.
1101 Monroe Street, Gretna, Louisiana 70053

To Scott and Susie,
who were married in Charleston

Acknowledgments

Many smoothed my way and in particular I'd like to thank: Beverly Foster at The Charleston Museum; Ann Fox at The Joseph Manigault House; Frank McGuire for his interest, suggestions, and editorial input; Moakler Processing Service of Atlanta for their flawless E6 processing; Tim Pollard for his photographic assistance; Jan Arrington for computer formatting; museum curators and administrators, plantation owners, restaurant and inn managers, college administrators, and especially the owners of these special homes who gave graciously of their time and made many helpful recommendations.

Contents

Introduction

Fashioned by three hundred years of rich history, Charleston resembles a prized, bejeweled pendant on a necklace formed by the Ashley and Cooper Rivers.

The first permanent settlers came to this region from England by way of Barbados. Under the command of William Sayle, they faced the perils of the Atlantic Ocean and finally made landfall off the Carolina coast in 1670. Guided upriver by friendly Kiawah Indians, they established a settlement which they called Charles Towne Landing. Land was allocated by the Lord Proprietors and plantations were started by families whose wealth and power eventually grew throughout the Low Country. In the Spring of 1680 the colonists relocated on Oyster Point, a peninsula between the Ashley and Cooper Rivers. Surveyor-General Maurice Mathews planned the "Grand Modell": a walled town with wide streets, spaces for churches, public buildings, and one hundred wooden dwellings. From this humble beginning Charleston was established.

Shortly afterwards, French Huguenots arrived under the leadership of Rene Petit. These Protestants were fleeing persecution after the revocation of the Edict of Nante and came with the blessing of King Charles II of England, who subsidized their passage. He let it be known their skills producing oils, making wine, brick-making, weaving, and farming would benefit his colony. The 1690s brought hurricanes, a smallpox epidemic, fire, and yellow fever, all of which killed many colonists.

During the eighteenth century the Province was fighting Indians, French, Spanish, and pirates who looted and sank supply ships. William Rhett pursued the pirates and brought them back to Charles Towne for justice. Forty-six pirates were hanged, including their notorious leader "Gentleman Pirate" Stede Bonnet.

Religious freedom attracted many diverse religious groups to the Carolina Province. Huguenots came in large numbers, settling Low Country plantations, and Episcopalians established their religion as early as 1670. Congregationalists and Presbyterians were united in 1690, and Scottish Presbyterians separated and formed the Scots Kirk. Jews, Lutherans, and Methodists also practiced their faiths unimpeded, and by 1786 a Roman Catholic Mass had been celebrated in the city.

In 1720 settlers repudiated the Lord Proprietor's rule and pledged allegiance to the King of England, becoming a Royal Colony. Ten years later Charles Towne entered its "Golden Age": years of extensive shipping and trade, reinforced by a rice and indigo culture. Elegant mansions began to appear and urban dwellings swelled the city. The first printing press was set up, and in 1734 Carolina's first newspaper, the Gazette, was published.

In 1740 a great fire destroyed three hundred buildings. Most of the southeastern section of the city was lost. It was then decided to build houses with spaces between them for safety. This saw the birth of the Charleston single house. These detached houses were constructed with their narrow end on the street. Only one room wide, and two or three rooms deep, a narrow side yard provided a fire-break. Grander double houses, constructed on larger lots, had two rooms facing the street divided by a front entrance and hallway. These building concepts dominated house design in Charleston for three hundred years. Early houses were renovated to keep pace with fashions, and as a result we now see Palladian, Georgian, Federal, Greek Revival, Rococo, and Victorian styles in the city's architecture. Sometimes several periods are mixed within the same building.

Evidence of locally made bricks can be seen in even the earliest buildings. Referred to as either Low Country or Cooper River brick or Charleston gray brick, they were used in construction from about 1690. Particularly fine examples are Boone Hall Plantation's "Slave Street" and other out-buildings constructed from early bricks made by slaves. Later, many brick houses were covered in stucco after repeated hurricanes and particularly after the earthquake of 1886. Evidence of cracks could be hidden, but the tell-tale reinforcing bolts show the extent of the damage.

As prosperity grew in the Province, homes became more opulent and many successful planters, merchants, and bankers constructed their townhouses with imaginative flamboyance. Influenced by changing architecture in England, prominent citizens built grand mansions with courtyards, carriage-houses, servant's quarters, and gardens. London Magazine wrote of Charles Towne in 1762, "Here the rich people have handsome equipages; the merchants are opulent and well bred; the people are thriving and extensive, in dress and life; so that everything conspires to make this town the politest, as it is one of the richest in America."

The next decade saw increasing resentment against the mother country. In 1773, a cargo of tea was taken from ships in the harbor and stored in the Exchange Building's basement to prevent paying British Government taxes. Unlike Boston's "Tea-party," Charleston's tea was kept dry and later sold to help fund the Revolution. Revolutionary feeling ran high, and in 1775 Lord William Campbell, last Royal Governor, fled the city in the dead of night, taking the great seal of the Province with him. Thus ended Royal Government in South Carolina. British Parliament declared the Colonies in rebellion, and in 1776 the Provincial Congress assembled in the Exchange Building and adopted a constitution establishing the First Independent Government in America. Arthur Middleton, Thomas Lynch Jr., Thomas Heyward Jr., and Edward Rutledge were local figures who signed the Declaration of Independence.

With the advent of war, a British fleet of 270 guns attacked but failed to take Fort Moultrie. In 1778 the British attacked again overland from Savannah. The city held but surrounding lands were torched. John Rutledge became Governor and Commander-in-Chief of American Revolutionary forces, "To do for public good" and acquired the nick-name "Dictator John." In February 1780 General Sir Henry Clinton attacked by land and sea, and the British seized control of the harbor, taking John's Island with 11,000 men. On May 12, 1780, local commander General Benjamin Lincoln surrendered his American force of 5,000 men, and Charles Towne was occupied.

Many prominent leaders were arrested and exiled to St. Augustine. As resistance grew, Francis Marion, "The Swamp Fox," harassed the British in the interior while Governor Rutledge kept revolutionary feelings alive. One autumn night in 1782 the cry rang out in the city streets, "Half-past twelve of a stormy night, and Cornwallis has surrendered." One year later, unable to control the rebellious Province, the British left Charles Towne and a triumphant American army marched in.

In 1783, Charles Towne changed its name to Charleston and a City Government was established. In May of 1788 delegates met in the Exchange Building for the Ratification Convention attended by many local dignitaries. South Carolina became the eighth state to ratify the U.S. Constitution.

The next ten years saw decline. Fires were a persistent problem and sometimes firemen resorted to gunpowder to stop the flames. Thousands were left homeless. Even the Huguenot church was a casualty. Some good things did happen, however. George Washington visited in 1791 and was welcomed with great pomp on his Southern tour. Also, an event took place that affected the city's architectural future. Dominican French Roman Catholic settlers evacuated Haiti due to slave uprisings. They brought their idea of galleries with them to Charleston and these became the famous piazzas. Strategically placed and accompanied by tall windows and high ceilings, the piazza changed life in the humid summer climate. Attracted by the prospect of cooler temperatures, plantation families vacated to the city in summer. "King Cotton," the plantations' new cash crop, created a newfound prosperity, and Charleston, with help from the newly opened Santee Canal, re-established itself as a port, shipping huge cargoes to the north and Europe. Wealthy planters and merchants built new, elegant townhouses in the latest architectural styles, and population figures rose to 20,000.

During this affluent period, as many as 130 cabinet makers plied their trade in Charleston. Charleston-made furniture became much sought after for its quality craftsmanship. Mahogany from the West Indies and local cedar woods were both used in house construction and furniture-making. A mahogany mill was built and other rarer woods such as walnut came from upcountry. Most famous of all the cabinet makers was Thomas Elfe. Identified by his distinctive signature patterns, his furniture is on display in many museum houses today.

In the early 1800s the port declined as cotton lands were exhausted and the time of deceptive ease came to an end. The "Great Panic" of 1837 saw prices plummet and fortunes lost. Economic depression set in, affecting planters, merchants, and shippers. Charleston's recovery was marginal, but by 1839 the first high school was built and a railroad to Columbia was completed. By 1850 Charleston ranked third among southern cities in manufacturing behind Richmond and New Orleans.

"At 1:15 o'clock on December 20, 1860, unanimously the Ordinance of Succession was passed," read the Charleston Gazette news-sheet. This led to war between the states. The Secession Conference arrived in town the next year, and Citadel cadets prevented the Federal ship "Star of the West" from relieving Fort Sumter in Charleston Harbor. The first shots of the Civil War rang out. General Beauregard prepared the Confederate defense of the city, and a three-year Union blockade followed. On December 11, 1861, a great "Hurricane Fire" swept the city, destroying everything in its path. Charleston was besieged by man and nature.

The following year the world's first submarine, "H.L.Huntly," sank a Federal frigate and the newly invented semi-submersible torpedo boat "David" harassed Federal ships, thus preventing a frontal attack from the harbor. A Federal bombardment followed in August 1863 and continued more than fifty days. Sherman's troops ransacked and torched plantations in outlying districts. In February 1865, city lines to the interior were cut, the Confederates evacuated, and victorious Union soldiers marched into a barren city. In May of that year an earthquake killed one hundred people and homes were left derelict.

After the Civil War Charlestonians were too poor to remodel their homes, so buildings retained their distinctive old charm and tradition. During this period, the local saying "too poor to paint, too proud to whitewash" came into being. Recovery came when Charleston was chosen to be a major naval base, as industry soon followed. After decades of poverty and peeling paint a clean-up began. Preservationists fought to prevent indiscriminate demolition, and a move was made to save the city. On October 13, 1931, the City Council adopted a proposal outlining 144 acres a Historic District, which formed the nation's first Historic City Government Ordinance. In 1947, The Historic Charleston Foundation was formed. They bought the Nathaniel Russell House and also saved slum neighborhoods, restoring more than sixty homes. In 1968 they began commercial restoration projects and co-sponsored the Broad Street beautification program. The restoration of boutiques, restaurants, and inns on King Street continues, and the $85 million Charleston Place and Omni Hotel now draw thousands of visitors.

Hurricane Hugo hit the South Carolina coast with a vengeance in 1989. Most of Charleston lost its roofs, many houses were flooded, and water damage from wind and rain lashing through broken windows spoiled decor and furnishings. The damage was particularly significant to property facing open water. But Charlestonians are familiar with disaster and boast "despite decease, fire, flood, war, an earthquake, recession, and hurricanes our city has survived." They picked up, repaired, and repainted.

This jewel of a city still sparkles.

The Majesty of Charleston

Boone Hall Plantation

Mount Pleasant

Major John Boone accompanied the "First Fleet" of settlers from England in 1681 and received this land as a grant from the Lords Proprietors. Boone Hall began growing rice, but later became a prosperous cotton plantation covering 17,000 acres. The locally famous Cooper River gray bricks were made here and all the utility buildings, walls, paths, and the present mansion are constructed from them. A working plantation for three hundred years, Boone Hall established pecan groves in 1904 and still produces a commercial crop.

The earlier house was replaced by this antebellum Georgian mansion in 1935 and is constructed entirely of plantation-made bricks in a beautiful garden setting.

In 1743 Capt. Thomas Boone laid out this long oak-lined drive leading to the house. This avenue together with a smokehouse and slave cabins are listed in the Register of Historic Places.

Unusual garden walls made from old plantation bricks.

"Slave Street" (ca. 1743). Nine brick-built slave cabins, unique in the United States.

Magnolia Plantation and Gardens

Ashley River Road

White lattice bridges connect pathways winding through the gardens.

Thomas Dayton arrived here from Barbados in 1671 and married Ann Fox. Together the newlyweds established Magnolia Gardens which became the plantation estate where nine generations of South Carolina's eminent Drayton family have lived.

The house together with five hundred acres of lawns, gardens, marshes, and trails are open to visitors who experience picturesque views at every turn. An eighteenth century Herb garden as well as a Topiary garden, a Biblical garden, and a petting zoo for children add enjoyment. A wildlife observation tower overlooks a waterfowl refuge with canoe trails through the marshlands.

This is the third house to stand at Magnolia. The first, a grand mansion thought to be a copy of Drayton Hall in England, burned in 1810 and the second was torched by Sherman's troops in 1865. Age unknown, this house was moved from Summerville by Rev. John Ginske Drayton and placed on burned foundations. After his death in 1891 his daughter Julia added the living room, dining room, and water tower.

Cypress trees stand reflected in still-water pools.

Renowned azaleas, first planted by Rev. John Grimke Drayton, blaze their colors in 250 varieties.

This bright and airy living room displays the tasteful pleasures of both nineteenth and twentieth century life, combining wicker and hand-painted furniture. The rug is Persian (ca. 1870).

This tiny bedroom contains many family mementos and Victorian furniture in Mahogany.

The dining room table is set with Drayton family's Chinese "Lowestoft" china collection. Seventy-one pieces have survived and are on display. The dining chairs are Hepplewhite and a pedestal table under the far window is a Duncan Phyfe.

The master bedroom furniture is all hand-painted in matching flower motif and has a matching wardrobe on an opposite wall.

Audubon Swamp Gardens

This cypress and tupelo swamp rises from sixty acres of black water adjoining Magnolia Plantation. A boardwalk reaches out into this eerie beauty spot.

Drayton Hall

3380 Ashley River Road

Built between 1738 and 1742 Drayton Hall is now a property of the National Trust for Historic Preservation. A fine example of Colonial American architecture it is constructed in the unusually sophisticated early Georgia Palladian style clearly built to impress. This country estate was not a plantation but a place where John Drayton, who owned many plantations, made his home. Through seven generations of Drayton ownership the house has remained in virtually original condition and is the only Ashley River house to survive the Civil War. Its unique state of unrestored preservation and rich hand-crafted details offer a rare glimpse of early Southern lifestyle. Local materials were used in its construction together with white English limestone and West Indian Mahogany. Still without modern amenities, this grand unfurnished showplace is open to visitors throughout the year.

This house stands as a tribute to the skills of African slaves of the period, without whose efforts many of these fine buildings would not have been possible.

Ionic pilasters support moldings in candlewick and dart, egg and dart as well as many other designs.

Close inspection reveals outstanding elaborate craftsmanship. Ceiling designs, which are repeated over the magnificent mantle, were carved into wet plaster.

Middleton Place
Ashley River Road

Henry Middleton, grandson of an early settler, himself a land owner both in South Carolina and England by inheritance, married wealthy heiress Mary Williams in 1741. Henry's dowry was the house and plantation he and Mary called Middleton Place, a particularly valuable track of land because of its elevation over the Ashley River flood plane. Influenced by the impressive gardens of Europe, Henry created a garden like no other in the thirteen colonies. The terraced lawns were laid out, and ponds and walkways constructed, offering exceptional vistas over the surrounding Low Country.

Henry held many important colonial posts until his opposition to British policy lead him to be elected the President of the First Continental Congress. At the time he owned 50,000 acres that supported about 800 slaves. His son Arthur inherited the plantation after his father's death. Said to be a cultured man he was a signer of the Declaration of Independence.

Arthur's son was the next Henry Middleton and it was he who turned Middleton Place into a horticultural paradise. With the help of his friend French botanist Andre Michaux, they introduced exotic plants such as camellias to American soil. This Henry also served a term as Governor of South Carolina, ten years in both houses of State legislature, and was America's minister to Russia.

William Middleton was the next owner and introduced azaleas to his property in great numbers. He also signed the Ordinance of Secession, and helped the Confederate cause in their defense of Charleston. On February 22, 1865 Sherman's troops put Middleton Place House to torch and ransacked family books, paintings, and treasures, leaving the mansion in ruins.

All that remains today is the south flanker of the original house. Salvaged after the Civil War and restored in the 1920s, the house contains abundant family furniture, silver, china, paintings, books, and documents.

Portraits of four generations of Middletons are displayed in the living room. A 1771 Benjamin West painting of baby Henry with his parents hangs over the Chinese Chippendale fretwork breakfast table, attributed to Charleston cabinet maker Thomas Elfe.

An English secretary bookcase (ca. 1790) is in an archive room displaying family treasures among which is a silk copy of the Declaration of Independence.

The silver Epergne on the family dining table was made in London for Arthur Middleton.

The Music room features Empire style furniture made in Philadelphia in 1815, a departing gift from the Russians when the second Henry Middleton left St. Petersburg where he served as America's minister.

The French gold tiara with amethyst center stone and aquamarine clusters worn by Henry's wife at social affairs in Russia in the 1820s.

Schadow's marble "Wood Nymph" (ca. 1810) graces a quiet place in the formal gardens famous for japonicas and gorgeous azaleas.

An English bracket clock sits on this beautiful mahogany desk inlaid with holly wood (ca. 1800).

The north bedroom decorated for summer. A Charleston-made rice bed with a mosquito net valance is pulled away from walls for better air circulation. Light curtains and straw matting complete the cooling effect.

The winter bedroom on the north side of the house also has a Charleston rice bed (ca. early 1800s) and a gold silk suit displayed was found with other Middleton clothes in the camphorwood-lined leather trunk opened in the nineteenth century.

Middleton Place

Eliza's House

The newly opened Eliza's House (ca. 1870s) is a living microcosm of slave accommodation on the plantation. Eliza Leach was the last African American to live in the house referred to as the "Palace." She resided here 40 years and died in 1986 at the age of ninety-four. Susan Middleton wrote in 1882 of her loyal former slaves now freed and living in the "Palace."

Furnished with only the simplest necessities, and a mattress thrown on the floor serves as a bed.

Charleston Museum—Apothecary Shop

360 Meeting Street

Charleston Museum was founded in 1773, making it the oldest museum in America. Its exhibits preserve the social and natural history of the region including archaeology, ethnology, and ornothogy. There is also a large historic silver collection and a children's discovery room.

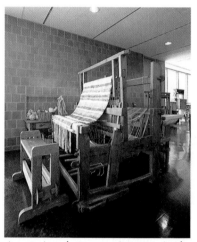

Displayed outside the museum is a full-scale replica of the Confederate submarine "H.L. Huntley" which was built in Charleston.

A weaving demonstration area in the museum.

This Apothecary shop is a microcosm of trade as it developed in this city. Established in 1780 on the corners of Broad and King Streets, a drug store remained open on that site until 1960. Pharmaceuticals were prescribed and dispensed by many professions other than physicians and it was not until the late eighteenth century that regulations prevailed. The items on display were gathered from collections and other shops in the area and represent two hundred years of history.

The house at 106 Broad Street that was an apothecary shop from 1780 until 1960.

Heyward-Washington House

87 Church Street

This grand Charleston double house was built in 1772 by Col. Daniel Heyward, a wealthy rice planter. The next year Thomas Heyward Jr. a signer of the Declaration of Independence, took up residence to conduct his law practice. The city leased the house for George Washington's stay when he visited in 1791. Heyward's aunt also ran a girls school here until 1794. The property passed to a judge, then became a boarding house and afterwards a bakery. A plate-glass window was installed and bread was made in the outside kitchen at the back. In 1929 Charleston Museum acquired and restored the property opening it as the city's first museum house. Today the house contains a valuable collection of eighteenth century Charleston-made furniture. It was designated a National Historic Landmark in 1978.

The formal garden is maintained by the Garden Club of Charleston.

This out-house kitchen dates back to 1740. Before the present house was built a gunsmith owned a small dwelling and shop on the property.

The dining room is at the rear near the kitchen. Chairs carved for Charles Pinkney are set around a drop leaf table next to a lockable sugar box. Daniel Heyward is pictured above the fireplace, which is original to the house.

The library contains the famous Holmes bookcase made between 1730–1775, considered one of the best American-made pieces of furniture existing today.

A large drawing room is furnished with a French spinet, a Venetian marble top table from Drayton Hall and Scalamandra drapes. The clock was locally made (ca. 1750) and a center table is by Thomas Elfe.

The guest bedroom's four-poster bed is carved in feather patterns and a beautiful wood-grain linen press and dressing table are Charleston-made. Matching tester, bed cover, and drapes were made specially for this room.

This Thomas Elfe bed with its unusual ball and claw feet design will break down for easy transportation. The chest-on-chest piece is also for traveling, again with the Elfe design front decoration.

This beautiful Charles Towne-made Joshua Lockwood clock still strikes the hour and shows the day of the month. In the background is the famous Holmes bookcase.

A library case of solid mahogany attributed to Robert Walker, a famous Charleston cabinet maker.

This skillfully worked desk with mirrored bookcase has the name William Axson carved in its bottom drawer, presumably the maker. Few signed pieces exist because labels were stuck on and insects ate the glue.

Joseph Manigault House
350 Meeting Street

When built in 1803, this elegant Federal style house was in a suburb called Waggborough. Joseph Manigault, a wealthy descendant of influential Huguenots, commissioned his brother Gabriel, an accomplished amateur architect, to build a town house befitting a successful plantation owner. The result was this splendid symmetrical Adamesque brick mansion. With emphasis on high ceilings, spacious interiors, and many tall windows, this house is wholly suited to Charleston's climate. Charleston Museum now owns this National Historic Landmark.

A large hallway with sweeping staircase, central focus of this priceless mansion.

This delicately furnished drawing room is upstairs. The painting is of Charles Manigault and his wife Elizabeth overlooking the Tiber River in Rome (ca. 1831).

A pair of pre-Revolutionary tilt-top tables with silver inlay centers displayed in a bay window.

Dining room chair backs have the crest of the pre-Revolutionary Governor of South Carolina, Mathews, inlaid in sterling silver. A clock on the mantle appears in the painting of Peter Manigault, both acquired by him on a visit to London in 1763.

In the card room, a Napoleon period French mahogany writing table with Egyptian influenced decoration of bronze dipped in gold.

This rice bed of local design with its original period tester would have been drawn to the room's center on hot nights.

A comfortable sitting area for winter nights by a fire.

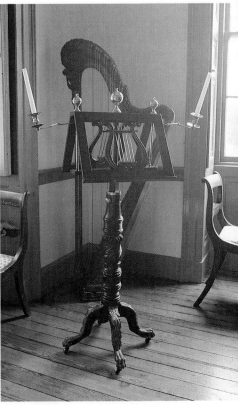

The famous Charleston-made linen press by cabinet maker Robert Walker (ca. 1810). This piece has its original maker's label intact, very rare from that period.

This unusual double-sided music stand has claw feet and candle sticks and is locally made. Behind is a nineteenth century French harp.

Aiken-Rhett House

48 Elizabeth Street

In 1817 John Robinson, a wealthy merchant, built this house in an uncorporated section of the city. It was an Adamesque style three-story double house on a raised basement, with sandstone steps from its main entrance onto Judith Street. A back coachyard was flanked by outbuildings. In 1825 John Robinson lost five ships at sea and sold the house to settle cargo losses.

William Aiken bought the house to use as a rental property. He was a successful cotton merchant who is best remembered as founder of the South Carolina Canal and Railroad Company. The city of Aiken, South Carolina is named after him. Upon his death in 1831, his son, also William, inherited this house, together with seven plantations, other rentals, and nearly one million dollars in cash. His vast holdings and wealth allowed him to maintain his position during the Civil War and he became first Governor of South Carolina in the 1840s and served in the U.S. Congress in the 1850s.

Double parlors are divided by large mahogany double doors. The Aiken family live here for fifty-five years during which time they remodeled the house in Greek Revival style and went to Europe on a shopping spree. They adorned their home with Empire furniture, Italian black marble fireplaces, and art. Lavish entertainers, the Aikens gave a reception with 500 guests for President Jefferson Davis.

A double flight of marble stairs ascend from the main entrance. General Beauregard moved his headquarters here for safety during the bombardment of 1863.

The heavy, mahogany dining room table was made by Joseph Meaks of New York in 1835. Henrietta Aiken, an only daughter, married Major Bernard Rhett, and one of their descendants continued living here until 1972.

Both bedrooms have similar "Sleigh-back" beds. Furniture dates about 1840 and is from New York. The condition of the decor throughout the house is exactly as it was when the Charleston Museum took over care of the property in 1975 after it had been abandoned. There are no plans to restore.

Most of the house was closed up in 1952 and remains without modern conveniences today. Electricity was installed but not in the main rooms.

A pretty dressing table was Henrietta's.

A bathroom with hot water pipes and portable toilets in closets (ca. 1910).

The Rococo gallery with the Aiken family art collection.

One of the few courtyards in the city still intact. Servant's quarters, stables, out-houses, and kitchen are exactly as they were left, showing the enormity of this property.

Massive piazzas on the south elevation catch the breezes and help to cool the interior.

Nathaniel Russell House

51 Meeting Street

Unlike most Charleston houses, this magnificent Federal period mansion sits back off the street in its own garden. It was built in 1808 for wealthy merchant Nathaniel Russell, who hailed from Rhode Island. The house served as his family home until his death in 1819. His youngest daughter lived here until 1857, whereupon it sold to Gov. Robert F.W. Allston. During the Civil War

A formal garden features plants typical of the 1820s.

Gen. Robert E. Lee was entertained here. After the war a school for girls was opened and later the house served as a convent school. Returning to a private residence in 1908 it remained so until the Historic Charleston Foundation purchased the property and opened this museum house in 1956.

An English silver epergne (ca. 1760), and Chinese porcelain in a "Sacred Butterfly" pattern grace the Charleston-made Hepplewhite dining table (ca. 1800). Local cabinetmakers made the sideboard also.

The oval second floor music room features a painting of Arthur Middleton. Window surrounds are elaborately carved in motifs picked out in gold. The classically inspired sofa was made in New York and the harp is French by Sebastien Erard of Paris (ca. 1803).

This downstairs elliptical library is furnished mostly with eighteenth century English pieces. Above the mantle is a portrait of Nathaniel Russell painted by Edward Savage in 1787.

A famous free-flying staircase built on the cantilever principle is the center of attention. The full length picture of Mary Rutledge Smith by London artist George Romney was painted in 1786.

In the upstairs Green Drawing Room with tall windows overlooking the street, the extent of elaborate carved wood molding and delicate elongated proportions of the Federal style can be seen. Fine plaster work around ceiling and mantle are typical of the period. The Charleston-made Hepplewhite Pembroke table is set with a Vieux Paris porcelain tea service.

Edmondston-Alston House

21 East Bay Street

This fine, solid Federal style house was erected in 1828 for Charles Edmondston who came from the Shetland Isles in Scotland. The second son of a physician, he became a wealthy shipping company owner. Suffering financial loss when cotton prices dropped in 1837 he sold out and returned to Europe.

Charles Alston, a rice planter from Georgetown County, bought the property as his town house and transformed it into a fashionable Greek revival mansion. He added a third floor and proudly placed his family crest in the decorative front parapet. An only daughter, Susan Pringle, never married and willed the house to her cousin Judge Henry Augustus Middleton Smith and his son. Thus the property entered into the family that also owns Middleton Place Plantation.

This morning room has mostly Alston family furniture which spans nearly 100 years. The desk is pre-Revolutionary (ca. 1770) and the red tub chairs are Victorian. The unusual wallpaper with flocked borders is copied from 1830 patterns when the introduction of chemical dyes gave very bright colors.

A Duncan Phyfe centerleaf dining table is set with George III English silver. The side board silver is Philadelphia-made (ca. 1800). The Regency Girondole with candlesticks was used to intensify the candlelight.

Two entrance doors exist. One leads from the piazza into the hall and the original front door opens into this charming reception room.

A very large hallway with sliding doors leads to the staircase. Displayed are prints, part of an extensive collection of Italian copper plate engravings.

Two tasteful drawing rooms separated by an unusual "Entra Salle," a later alteration in keeping with the Greek revival style. The English porcelain tea service belonged to Mrs. Alston and the harp is French (ca. 1811).

The oldest piece of furniture is this English desk in the library. Suitable for travel, the chest lifts from its legs (ca. 1730).

Once a gentleman's withdrawing room, the library contains family books and mementos. An original leather chair is the sign of a wealthy merchant.

Magnificent views of Charleston Harbor can be seen from these piazzas where lavish entertainment took place in the nineteenth century. On the lower piazza, one of the famous Charleston "Joggling Boards" designed in the 1830s for relaxation and mild exercise.

Calhoun Mansion

16 Meeting Street

This splendid Italian-style mansion was built between 1876 and 1878 by George Watson Williams, a local banker. The services of architect W.P.Russell were employed to design this house with 35 rooms containing 24,000 square feet of living space. Built of small red bricks laid in running standard bond, unusual for Charleston's antebellum buildings, the house has three front bays. The central bay incorporates an impressive main entrance of heavy cathedral doors under a two-tiered portico supported by Corinthian columns. Entry is by a double flight of steps leading to a foyer paved in colored tiles. Here

walnut panels with Trinity symbols inlaid in satin wood continue into a great hallway sixty-five feet long.

Upon Mr. Williams' death this property passed to his son-in-law Patrick Calhoun, a grandson of the famous John C. Calhoun, Vice President of the United States and Great Nullifier. Several owners followed until in 1976 the present owner purchased the mansion and lavishly restored and furnished it.

Sumptuous is the only description for the inside of this show house. Parquet, tiled, and carpeted floors, painted and molded ceilings, paneled and papered walls, real marble, rich furnishings and fabrics, and exquisite chandeliers adorn every room.

Victoriana at its best, the drawing room's Louis XIV furniture, Italian chandeliers, and English paintings are perfect.

A small, elaborate reception room just inside the front door.

The library with a Louis XIV desk, and tiles depicting Shakespearean plays around the fireplace.

Victorian ladies and gentlemen gathered separately. This was the ladies' sitting room with dividing doors into the library.

The walnut staircase leads to fifteen bedrooms, all with their own full bathrooms.

A statue guards the stairway in the second floor hall.

The dining room invites banqueting in grand style. The table is original to the house (ca. 1875), and has a rosewood top on a mahogany pedestal. English chairs (ca. 1885) are restored with new leather and the owner's monogram. Thirty-two rectangles on the ceiling each have a cluster of fruit covered in gold leaf. The silver collection is English and American.

This beautiful vase is Meissen porcelain (ca. 1835).

This heavy bed of inlaid oak is three hundred years old.

A guest-room bed with half tester.

The skylight in this gallery, with pink motif, is forty-five feet high.

Old Exchange Building & Provost Dungeon

122 East Bay Street

Early Charles Towne settlers built a Court of Guard here where Indians and pirates, including Stede Bonnet, were imprisoned. Town meetings were held in a hall above. Builders Messrs. John and Peter Holbeck were contracted to construct the Exchange Building which they completed in 1771. With striking Palladian architecture and a Portland stone facade, the building dominated the harbor which it served as a trading exchange and customs house.

This historic "Great Hall," the exchange's assembly room, is where citizens protested the Tea Act in 1773 and subsequently stored the tea in the cellar. South Carolina's delegates to the Continental Congress of 1774 were elected here and two years later South Carolina declared its independence from Britain on the steps outside. Col. Isaac Hayne the patriot was imprisoned in the back room with his coffin, before being executed by the British for treason. In 1791 President George Washington visited Charleston, and a great gala concert and ball was held here in his honor.

Once a Post Office, this room is used for meetings by Daughters of the American Revolution. Prized furniture collected since they took over care of the Exchange in 1913 include the odd array of "Personal" chairs brought to meetings by individual members.

In early 1780 General Moultie hid 10,000 lbs. of powder belonging to besieged Charleston, bricking up the barrels behind a false wall in this vaulted basement. The occupying British made this their dungeon for two and a half years without discovering the gunpowder cache. From this prison pirates have been taken to hang, and later Revolutionary leaders were incarcerated. In 1960 part of Charles Towne sea wall was excavated here under a section called "Half-Moon Battery" and is now on display.

Powder Magazine

79 Cumberland Street

The Province was protecting itself from frequent Indian, Spanish, French, and pirate attacks, so in 1703 the Common House of Assembly authorized a brick powder house to be built. This unusual building was constructed with thirty-two-inch thick walls in a unique eight gable structure for strength. Still occupying its original site, it formed the northern boundary of a fortification wall surrounding the small town.

The National Society of the Colonial Dames of America in the State of South Carolina purchased this building for their headquarters in 1902 and its restoration was the first such project in Charleston. It was designated a National Historic Landmark in 1989.

Museum showing early Colonial artifacts.

This old iron door was the original entrance.

This dress was made with silk from a Low Country plantation.

Thomas Elfe House
54 Queen Street

A delightful Charleston single house in miniature, the Thomas Elfe house contains original woodwork by the famous local cabinet maker and reproductions of his furniture designs. Built originally on the street about 1760, the house was moved back to its present site when restored. Heavy beams joined by wooden pegs helped this exceptionally sturdy structure to withstand the earthquake of 1886. This private residence, now open for guided tours, is registered in the Historical American Building Survey, U.S. Dept. of Interior.

Throughout the house, fireplaces, paneling, and doors are made of cypress wood which was originally painted. Several coats of paint were removed during restoration, exposing eighteenth century craftsmanship.

The comfortable family room contains showcased memorabilia. Thomas Elfe moved on to grander homes as his prosperity grew, but here in these tiny rooms is his legacy.

The front bedroom is decorated and furnished as in Elfe's day.

A collection above the narrow stairway shows the kind of hand tools used by Thomas Elfe. His surviving account books for 1768–1775 are now with the Charleston Library Society and show records for over 1500 pieces of cabinetwork made in his later years. Original examples of his furniture are prized by museums and private collectors throughout the city. Distinctive fretwork patterns, leg designs, and inner-draw construction identify this renowned furniture maker's craftsmanship.

Beds were custom-made to fit both the room and person. Their height matched the window sills to catch breezes.

Dock Street Theatre
135 Church Street

A theatre was built on Dock Street under the direction of Governor Rutledge, and opened on February 12, 1736 as the New Theatre in Dock Street. The production was a bawdy comedy titled "The Recruiting Officer." One month later Dock Street was changed to Queen Street but the theatre kept the old name. It is thought this building perished in the fire of 1740, and rumored that a second theatre was built in 1754 and was destroyed shortly thereafter. A theatrical troop, The American Company, contracted a new building which opened on December 5, 1763 but the Revolution overshadowed its success. Mysteriously, the building was gone when the lot was sold in 1781.

The Planter's Hotel was built on the site in 1800 and became a "Rendezvous of fashionable society in the antebellum South." The sandstone portico columns with their carved Barbados mahogany capital and cornices are from this period. More famous, the cast-iron balcony with its morning glory pattern was added in 1836. The Civil War closed the hotel, and a tornado struck, leaving only ancient local bricks and the imposing balcony.

Plans were drawn for a new theatre by architects Simons and Lapham utilizing existing structural features. The new theatre opened to a full house on November 26, 1937 with a production of "The Recruiting Officer" performed by the Footlight Players 201 years after the same play opened the original theatre in 1736.

The auditorium seats 463 people and has a parquet of thirteen boxes.

All the Adamesque woodwork, plaster work, and doors came from the Ratcliffe house (the old High School of Charleston), as did the gigantic gold mirror. The stairway and lobby area have been restored recently.

Pink House

17 Charmers Street

Built as a tavern in pre-Revolutionary times, the Pink House sits on a row in one of the few cobbled streets left in Charleston. With its durable walls of West Indian coral and ancient Spanish tiled roof this house, as legend claims, is where sailors drank grog in what was Mulath Alley, the red light district.

William Rhett House

54 Hasell Street

This dignified property is the oldest known house still standing in Charleston. This private residence was built after 1713 by William Rhett, Colonel in the Militia and Vice Admiral of the Province. He repulsed a French/Spanish attack in 1718 and later captured the notorious pirate Stede Bonnet. The house is also the birthplace of renowned Confederate Gen. Wade Hampton, who became Governor from 1876–79 and U.S. Senator from 1879–91.

French Triplet Houses

94–96–98 King Street

This distinctive row of attached brick houses were built about 1742 on land leased from the French Huguenot Church for ground rent. These dwellings of Cooper River bricks housed carpenters, watchmakers, a vintner, and a mariner. Later, a dance teacher held classes here. In one of these houses La Society Francaise de Bienaisance (French Society) was founded in 1816.

Rainbow Row

East Bay Street

Now painted in bright colors, these were among the city's first houses. Dating from the mid-1700s this attached, Northern European-style of building was abandoned in favor of the now famous detached Charleston single house because of frequent fires in the city.

St. Michael's Episcopal Church

78 Meeting Street

St. Michael's steeple is a distinctive landmark above Charleston. Established in 1751, the church's corner stone was laid the following year. After its inauguration in 1761, both President George Washington and Marquis de Lafayette worshiped here when visiting the city. Signers of the Constitution John Rutledge and Charles Cotesworth Pinckney are both buried in the graveyard. Its famous bells have crossed the Atlantic Ocean five times during their 200 year history.

First (Scots) Presbyterian Church

53 Meeting Street

Originally founded in 1731 by twelve Scottish families, Caledonian immigrants outside of the Anglican faith. Known as the Scots Kirk, this church was dedicated in 1814 and bears the seal of the Church of Scotland. President James Monroe worshiped here on May 2, 1819.

Du Bose Heyward House

78 Church Street

Du Bose Heyward, writer of "Porgy," later to become the famous "Porgy and Bess," lived in part of this house when it was a divided residence. He based his Catfish Row in the story on Cabbage Row, located less than a block north on Church Street and now a commercial property appropriately called Porgy and Bess.

Miles Brewton House

27 King Street

This fine house was built for Miles Brewton in 1769. Ezra Waite, the architect of this Georgian style Charleston double house, also carved the magnificent Portland stone pillars that support the portico. Sir Henry Clinton and Lords Rawdon and Cornwallis made this their home while occupying Charleston. Later Generals Hatch and Mead lived here after the Civil War.

A tall ironwork fence with Chiveaux de Frise (pirate spikes) atop, fronts the house to ward off intruders.

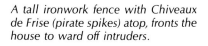

Market Hall
188 Meeting Street

This colorful building (ca. 1841) houses the Confederate Museum run by the Daughters of the Confederacy. A bustling Market Street runs east from here full of shops, boutiques, restaurants, and an extensive vegetable and souvenir market.

Fireproof Building
Corner of Meeting and Chalmers Streets

Designed by Washington Monument architect Robert Mills, this was the first fireproof building erected in the U.S. about 1826. It now houses the South Carolina Historical Society library.

Old Citadel

Marion Square

Built after attempted slave uprisings in 1822 and originally called the Arsenal, the Citadel housed troops and arms. Later the South Carolina Military Academy trained cadets here who in 1861 prevented the "Star of the West" from relieving Fort Sumter at the time of the Secession Convention.

Sword Gates

32 Legare Street

Exquisite sword gates were originally made for the Charleston Guard House, where the Post Office stands today. In 1830 iron worker Christopher Werner mistook an order for a pair of gates and made two pairs. Stored for 20 years, these extra gates were installed here by British Consulate George Hopley as a symbol of civic authority.

Hibernian Hall

105 Meeting Street

Home of the Hibernian Society, founded on March 17, 1801, this impressive building was completed in 1841.

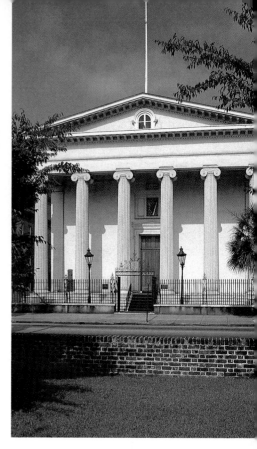

U.S. Customs House

200 East Bay Street

White Point Gardens

This Roman-Corinthian building of white marble was erected between 1849 and 1879 on the site of the old Craven Bastion. It was occupied by various government offices before becoming the U.S. Customs House.

Overlooking Charleston Harbor, White Point Gardens has been the peninsula's defense in storm and war. Once a place for executions and gun batteries, it stands now as a memorial to history.

East Battery

Houses on East Battery command a splendid view of Charleston Harbor.

Longitude Lane

Longitude Lane is an old cobbled street connecting East Bay with Church Street.

Confederate War Memorial

South Battery

This Confederate War Memorial overlooks Charleston Harbor and Fort Sumter.

Houses on South Battery are a delightful mixture of architectural styles.

Magnolia Cemetery

Historic Magnolia Cemetery, located on the banks of the Cooper River, is the burial place for generations of Southern leaders.

Old Santee Canal State Park
Moncks Corner

In 1773 excitement mounted when Henry Mouzon began to survey suitable waterways for digging a multiple lock canal connecting the Santee and Cooper Rivers. After intervention by Gov. Rutledge, Gov. William Moutree, and even George Washington, the Santee Canal was started in 1793 and began operation in 1800. On this pioneer project chief engineer Col. Christian Senf, a Swede, used 1000 slave laborers to dig and employed twenty-five carpenters to build locks. A profitable dividend-paying enterprise, the canal system recorded moving 80,000 bales of cotton and other goods in 1,720 boats from the Piedmont and central state region to the Port of Charleston.

A three-year drought between 1817 and 1819 dried up principle reservoirs where corn was then planted. Competition from newly introduced steamboat services and new railroads finally closed the canal in 1850.

Now open for public enjoyment, the Old Santee Canal State Park is located 25 miles outside Charleston.

60

Rutledge House Inn

116 Broad Street

John Rutledge built this house in 1763. Originally a two-story structure made of Low Country brick, successive owners have embellished the property. Most obvious is the iron work of Christopher Werner, who constructed elaborate decorative balconies, fences, stair-rails, and large pillars.

The house has a colorful history. It is said John Rutledge wrote much of the U.S. Constitution here. George Washington's diary shows he breakfasted here in 1791, and the Bishop of Charleston made it his home. Following the Civil War it was a U.S. District Courthouse and in the 1920s under the Mayor's ownership, George Vanderbilt and William Howard Taft were house guests. William Deas, butler at the time, devised Charleston's famous "She Crab Soup" on the premises.

After serving as a school, apartments, then a law office, local architects carefully restored this historic house in 1987, converting it into an inn.

Heart of the Inn, the drawing room is comfortably furnished for guests.

Centerpiece of the Elizabeth Grimke Suite is one of eight mantles located throughout the house, carved from Italian marble.

Palladian windows light the stairwell's exquisite parquet floors.

The entrance hall is flanked by Greek pilasters and the portrait is of John Rutledge.

Double fireplaces, a four-poster bed, and comfortable furniture are featured in the George Washington Suite.

Ashley Hall

172 Rutledge Avenue

This stately suburban Regency Villa on Rutledge Avenue was built by Patrick Duncan, a tallow-chandler and factor. The shell house was built by Charles Otto Witte when he lived here with his six beautiful daughters. In 1909 Dr. Mary Vardrine McBee opened her school for forty-five girl students. Today Ashley Hall is an all-girls independent day school.

Heavy Victorian moldings and decor dominate the drawing room.

Decorative moldings are everywhere in this vaulted upstairs hallway and stairs.

Extensive research went into the restoration of the Mildred Hubbard Board Room. Original ceiling designs were traced and faithfully reproduced by stenciling.

The spiral stairwell at Ashley Hall.

College of Charleston

66 George Street

The striking south elevation of Harrison Randolf Hall overlooks the campus of this nation's oldest municipal college. Founded in 1770 and chartered in 1785, the College of Charleston grew in reputation, and in 1828 this main building was erected. Designed by architect William Strickland in Classic Revival style, the simple two-story structure was later expanded. Additions of a portico with massive Roman Revival columns, extended wings, and an iron fence with porter's lodge that enclosed the campus, was undertaken by local architect Col. Edward Brickle White in 1850. He also designed Market Hall, the Huguenot Church, and St. Philip's Church Steeple. Randolf Hall now serves as the college administration building and has undergone extensive restoration.

The Alumni Room, supported by Doric columns.

The board room where administrators meet. Two large Ionic columns supporting a lintel divide a sitting area with pictures of past college presidents.

This impressive library-desk is in the President's office.

William Blacklock House

18 Bull Street

Harleston Village was open country bordering a tidal creek when this Adams style house was built for William Blacklock in 1800. Other houses followed, transforming the area into a fashionable suburb. Its impressive facade of Charleston gray brick is highlighted by a double-flight stairway of Portland stone and an iron balustrade, supported on marble columns.

The College of Charleston Foundation acquired this architectural treasure in 1971 and restored it shortly thereafter. Now home to the College's Club, it is used for various functions.

William Blacklock, a wealthy wine merchant, married into Napoleon's family. The drawing room reflects the French influence.

Exquisitely decorated, this upstairs dining room reflects the optimum atmosphere for elegant entertaining.

A wide hallway and impressive staircase divide this traditional double house.

The upstairs sitting room, a place for reflection.

St. Philip's Episcopal Church

142 Church Street

Founded in 1670, St. Philip's Church is the Mother Church of the Episcopal Diocese of South Carolina. The first church was built just inside the original walled city in 1680 on a site where St. Michael's Church now stands, and was known as the "English Church."

The second St. Philip's Church was built at its present location on Church Street, and the first services were held on Easter Sunday in 1723. Services continued for 112 years, during which time both President George Washington and John Wesley worshiped here.

Fire destroyed the building in 1835, but construction of the present church was begun immediately. Ser-

St. Philip's churchyard, located directly across Church Street, contains tombs of many historically well known city, state, and national leaders.

vices were first held in May 1838 and continued uninterrupted to the present day, except when the church was temporarily closed because of bombardment during the Civil War.

St. Philip's 200-foot landmark steeple has been used throughout history as a navigational aid to mariners. Designed by Edward B. White, the steeple originally housed a chime of eleven bells, but these were given to Confederate forces to smelt for cannons. Four bells and a ringing mechanism were installed in 1976.

Architect James Hyde used the classical Corinthian style when building the nave. He based his design on James Gibb's St. Martins-in-the-Fields in London. The present Chancel and Sanctuary were designed by Albert Simons following a fire in April 1920.

Circular Congregational Church

150 Meeting Street

In 1681 the original settlers of Charles Towne founded a Protestant or Dissenting church. They met in the "Old White Meeting House" on this site, which gave Meeting Street its name. In the 1700s as revolutionary sentiment spread, members and their minister William Tennant spoke out for political and religious freedom. When the British captured Charles Towne they set up a hospital in this place of worship and afterwards left it a shell. Members immediately began to rebuild their church. Martha Laurens Ramsey laid out a design for a circular church in 1804. Architect Robert Mills completed the plans for what was to be called "the most extraordinary building of its day."

In 1861 fire swept the city, gutting the "Old Circular." After the Civil War a much reduced congregation gathered up old bricks from the ruins and in 1890 raised a new Sanctuary in a Romanesque style. Inspired by Henry Hobart Richardson, the building incorporates two powerful forms, the circle outside and the shape of the Greek Cross inside.

In 1987 the Sanctuary was completely restored.

This exceptional tracker organ was built by George S. Hutchings of Boston and was installed in 1987.

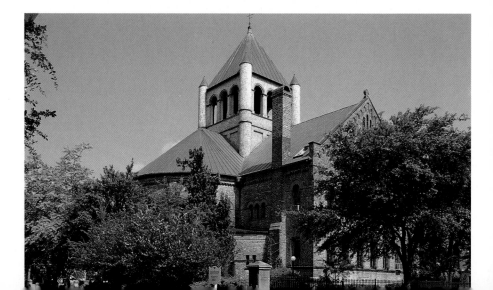

Beth Elohim Temple

86 Hasell Street

Members of the Jewish faith came to South Carolina as early as 1695. Sufficient numbers had gathered by 1749 to organize the present congregation Kahal Kadosh Beth Elohim (Holy Congregational House of God). In 1792 construction of a most impressive synagogue was begun and dedicated two years later. Unfortunately, this handsome Georgian building was destroyed by the great fire of 1838.

The massive ark is made of Santo Domingo mahogany. The stained glass windows showing Jewish religious symbols are replacements for those lost in the earthquake of 1886.

The present structure, a colonnaded temple after the finest example of Greek Revival architecture, was built and dedicated in 1841 on the same site. It was constructed by member David Lopez from designs by New York architect C.L. Warner. The original synagogue's foundation stone is installed over the entrance door in the foyer, and the original iron fence fronting the property was retained intact.

Unitarian Church
8 Archdale Street

Conceived as an expansion of the Independent Church in 1772, this building was nearly completed at the outbreak of the American Revolution. The British took the building over as militia quarters and stabled their horses in the sanctuary. After the war, the church was repaired and dedicated on October 25, 1787. The building was enlarged and remodeled between 1852 & 1854 when vaulted fantracery ceilings and fine stained glass windows were installed. The exterior was altered to a distinctive Gothic design with heavy buttresses and covered in stucco.

The sanctuary's vaulted ceiling bears unsupported plaster fantracery patterned after the Henry VII Chapel in Westminster Abbey.

St. Matthew's Lutheran Church

403 King Street

Patterned after a Lutheran church of ancient origin in northern Germany, St. Matthew's Church was completed in 1872. Dr. Louis Mueller, third pastor of the church, helped design this imposing structure which overlooks Marion Square with its 297-foot steeple.

In 1901 a clock and ten bells were installed in the tower, and after a great fire and subsequent restoration in 1965, three more were added. The present Austin organ consists of fifty-eight ranks of 3841 pipes plus chimes, harp, and cymbelstern.

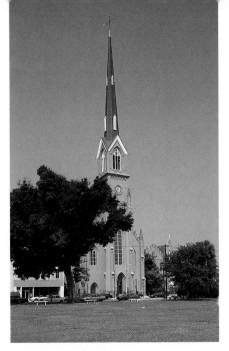

Impressive stained glass windows are replacements from after the fire. They were made by the German company of George Maier, who also made the magnificent windows behind the altar a century before.

The French Protestant Huguenot Church

136 Church Street

In 1680 the sailing ship "Richmond" brought instructions from England's King Charles II to name the new settlement Charles Towne. On that vessel also came forty-five French Protestant refugees fleeing France's religious persecution. King Charles subsidized the voyage to establish their skills of silk, oil, and wine-making into his colony. The Huguenot Church was founded and built in 1687 on its present site, which was then called Dock Street. Other Huguenots arrived and populated land adjoining the Cooper River, from where they would travel by boat to services timed to coincide with the tides.

On June 13, 1796 firemen "blew up" the church to help prevent a great city fire from spreading. The faithful were forced to worship elsewhere until, in 1800, the building was replaced. Poor attendance, sometimes without ministry, forced that church's closure and it was torn down in 1844. The following year, local architect Edward Brickle White and contractor Erphraim Curtis built the present church, which was Charleston's first Gothic structure.

The magnificent chandelier was "painted black to fool the Yankees" during the Civil War.

First Baptist Church

61 Church Street

A congregation of Baptists was formed about three years after the founding of Charles Towne under the leadership of Rev. William Screven who led a group fleeing persecution in New England. William Elliott donated the land and the First Baptist Church was erected in 1699. One of the most historic Charleston churches, the present building dates from 1826.

William Bull House

35 Meeting Street

This lot was granted to Stephen Bull of Ashley Hall and Sheldon. One of the oldest dwellings in the city, the house was built in 1720 by his son William Bull, who was Second Lieutenant Governor of South Carolina. There have been a variety of owners, and it is uncertain who added the piazzas, but the exterior remains virtually unchanged from the original.

Two flights of steps allow access on either side to the front door. It was from this elevated platform that Gov. Robert Y. Hayne dissuaded a group of nullificationists from proceeding to the Battery with intentions of seizing a ship and declaring war on the Union.

When the Hayne family resided here they ran a small school at the rear of the garden. One of their notable students, DuBose Heyward, later became author of the famed "Porgy and Bess."

This front living room was called the parlor in the old days. Folding campaign chairs from the Civil War flank the fireplace. Woodwork around the ceiling is the original.

The house is furnished with many reproduction pieces skillfully made by the present owner. The Pembroke table and block front sideboard are copies from originals in the National Metropolitan Museum. The wicker pram is a family heirloom from 1920, and a child's chair folds to become a rocker.

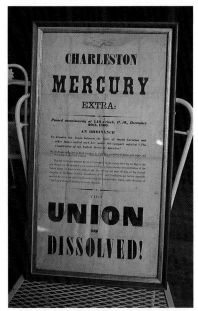

Much of the interior has been dramatically altered. Once enclosed, the staircase now descends directly into this large entrance hall furnished with a grand piano. Extra light is admitted through three Palladian windows.

A Charleston Mercury Extra Bulletin dated December 20, 1860 declares "UNANIMOUSLY AT 1:15 O'CLOCK THE ORDINANCE OF SECESSION WAS PASSED." This historic document belongs to the present owner.

Thomas Lamboll House
19 King Street

This King Street residence was built in 1735 for Thomas Lamboll by master carpenter and builder Thomas Lee. He drew up his own plans and constructed this strong wooden house after the fashion of shipbuilding of the day.

With its front door moved to an entryway when piazzas were added in the 1800s, this is a beautiful example of an early, rather large Charleston single house.

The ground floor piazza now used for relaxation.

Very large two-story piazzas were added to the south side to capture the breezes.

In an upstairs drawing room there is a decorative hand-chiseled gouge pattern on the woodwork, around windows, and chair rails.

A beautiful set of Chippendale Sentinel chairs stand around a flower ornamented dining table. Sheffield silver plate is displayed in cabinets, and an early 1800s English sideboard is carved in wheatsheaf patterns with lion's heads in brass. This originally had a headboard with cup hangers. A gold leaf screen is part of a Japanese collection in the house.

A downstairs drawing room features many interesting pieces collected by the present owners.

Thirty-six Meeting Street

36 Meeting Street

This lot was owned by A. Vanderhorst, a planter from Berkely County and then sold in 1743 to carpenter Easie Brunch. He was probably the builder of this excellent early example of a Charleston single house in Georgian style. The original woodwork is remarkable throughout this sound structure, which has survived the wrath of wars, fires, storms, and neglect for which Charleston's history is famous. Customary piazzas were added to the south side of the house as late as 1850, and the detached kitchen and stables were joined to become part of the main structure.

Now a guest room, the old kitchen still contains the original brick-built oven and fireplace, a rare find in this city.

Fretwork on the mantle in the living room is in the tradition of local cabinet maker Thomas Elfe. The fireplace itself is of Rumford design, famous for its maximum heat circulation. Rumford produced a noted book on this subject but later returned to England, being on the wrong side in the Revolution.

The dining table is a Duncan Phyfe reproduction, and the Hepplewhite sideboard with inlaid sandalwood was made in South Carolina in 1820. The Sheffield silver was made in 1850. On the mantle, a collection of Royal Crown Derby (ca. 1860) is displayed. A one hundred year old Chinese rug and a watercolor by Charleston artist Margaret Peery complete the decor.

Executive Headquarters House

37 Meeting Street

This early example of a pre-Revolutionary brick-built house was possibly built by James Simmons, who mentioned the house in his will of 1775, and construction is thought to date from 1750–1760. The property was seized during the British Occupation from its next owner, Gov. Robert Gibbs, and ransacked.

Ownership passed to William Bristane in 1782 and later to Otis Mills in 1846, who completely changed the character of this property. Additions included the unusually large bay fronts with tall beveled glass windows, decorative gables, and ironwork, and a magnificent entrance with heavy double doors under a New Orleans style balcony. The two-foot thick walls were covered with stucco.

Gen. Pierre Gustave Toutant Beauregard made this his Executive Headquarters House. From here he commanded his Confederate forces and organized the defense of Charleston. In 1863 a Federal bombardment drove the General back to a safer stronghold further north.

The double drawing room is delicately furnished in European style. Matching rugs are custom made in the Aubosson design.

Black and white marble flooring and silver, hand-painted wallpaper welcome visitors in the entrance hall. Impressive arched doorways lead to every room.

Close detail of plaster work in miniature Corinth columns and pilasters dividing the drawing room.

One of a pair of late nineteenth century French curio cabinets with decorative gold leaf.

The dining room set has leather-seated chairs. A centerpiece soup tureen is marked Villeroy & Boch, Mettlach and has a grapevine motif and a matching plate. The chest with brass handles is English (ca. 1820) and the sideboard is Hepplewhite.

An intricately carved Chinese screen in the dining room.

A richly decorated library extends into one of the front bays. The restored wooden mantle has delicate reeding and serpentine designs, and the hearth is Delft tiled.

Close view of the Delft tiled hearth in the library.

John Drayton House

Ladson Street

The exact date of this house cannot be established. John Drayton purchased the land in 1746 from his father-in-law, Lt. Gov. William Bull, and possibly built shortly afterwards. Originally constructed in Georgian style as a two-story structure, it has been remodeled twice. Before 1813 the bow fronted expansion was added and rooms were redecorated in the Federal, or Adams, style. Later the house was remodeled again after Colonial Revival styles.

Ladson Street was originally a lane cut through the William Bull property on Meeting Street to give access to this house. Early in the twentieth century it was widened and extended west to reach King Street.

A kitchen house on the side with servant quarters and a small garden was a separate building.

This view through the dining room, hall, and sitting room shows the inside width of the house. Arched doorways were installed about 1813. The silver and table are both English and an Adams mantle is made with two colors of Italian marble.

A massive Rococo Revival gold leaf mirror (ca. 1850) came from a local plantation house. An English tall-case clock on the stairs was made in 1700, and the banister rail is of mahogany.

The Adams mantle in the sitting room was found to have an exquisite grape and vine design after restoration. The sofa is Sheraton.

Once an upstairs sitting room, this bright and airy guest bedroom is in the front of the house. The frieze around the ceiling is original, and both beds are made of mahogany.

Daniel Elliott Huger House

34 Meeting Street

Captain John Bull built this fine three-story Charleston double house in the 1760s on land purchased from Indian trader George Eveleigh in 1759. Bull died leaving everything to his wife Mary. In 1775 Lord William Campbell, South Carolina's last Royal Governor, fled the colonies in the dead of night from this house, thus ending British Colonial rule.

Daniel Elliott Huger, who became a noted South Carolina legislator and jurist, bought the house in 1818. Marquis de Lafayette, a great friend of the Huger family, was entertained here when visiting Charleston.

The entrance hall is divided by an arch supported on fluted pilasters. An attractive staircase has a broad mahogany handrail and spindle-turned balusters.

Heavy triple piazzas and stucco were added to this enormous Carolina brick house, probably after the earthquake of 1886.

Rich reds dominate the dining room. The Charleston-made sideboard dates from 1800.

Upstairs, double drawing rooms extend the entire length of the second floor. Decorative plaster ceilings and distinguished carved wooden overmantles grace these exquisite period rooms.

A clock made by Isaac Rogers of London stands in the upstairs hall.

This charming fountain, a copy of "Ralph Izard as a little boy" (born 1717), was done by Elizabeth Sippen Green Elliott in 1942.

Daniel Ravenel House

68 Broad Street

Ravenels have lived here since 1735. Isaac Mazyck owned the property first, then it passed through his daughter Charlotte's marriage to Daniel Ravenel. This bonded the friendship of two Huguenot families that arrived on these shores together in 1685.

The first house burned down in 1796, but this well-proportioned Charleston single house was immediately erected in its place. Made of Low Country brick, marble keystones add strength to this solid three-story structure. Dutch glazed-brick window lintels, and decorative brickwork beneath eaves and parapet, give the facade distinction. Side piazzas have an open upper level with a beautifully carved balustrade. From here is a view of adjoining Washington Park. This house has survived earthquake, fire, and bombardment.

Arched doorways access both library and dining room from a side piazza entrance hall.

The library contains rare books of Huguenot and South Carolina history, some dating from 1686. Letters from George Washington, Lafayette, and Moultrie were found pressed between book pages. Charts, documents, and family memorabilia from a quarter of a century are here.

Furniture and china in the dining room is from Hounus Plantation. Family silver dates from 1771, and the sideboard is Empire (ca. 1820).

The upstairs drawing room has floor-to-ceiling cypress paneling and a beautifully carved mantle, now restored. The Empire couch is American-made (ca. 1810).

Close inspection of the hunting scene carved into the mantle.

Palmer House

5 East Battery

The prominent house overlooking Charleston Harbor known as the "Pink Palace" attracts many sightseers. This distinctive property was built in 1849 by John Ravenel with three foot thick Cooper River brick walls that have withstood both earthquake and hurricane. Double piazzas supported by large white columns overlook the harbor and a beautiful walled side garden.

John Ravenel was a physician and scientist. He invented phosphate fertilizer and the semi-submersable torpedo boat "David" which was used as a harbor defense during the Civil War.

The carpeted stairway has a carved mahogany handrail and stanchion.

The fireplace is black African marble with a painting "Head of St. John the Baptist" (Italian, ca. 1890) over the mantle.

The drawing room overlooking the harbor has fifteen-foot ceilings.

The smaller withdrawing room has a gilt mirror with bird and grape motif over its mantle, and an Oriental rug.

The dining room table is American-made (ca. 1790) and the chest opens into a standing butler's desk. A large mirror reflects a portrait of Mrs. Palmer, and hurricane shades on the mantle are etched with the American eagle.

William Pinckney Shingler House

9 Limehouse Street

This decorative Greek Revival mansion epitomizes the period's extravagances. Built in 1856, it was the brainchild of William Pinckney Shingler, but it is also suspected to be strongly influenced by local renowned architect Edward Brickle White. Despite the ornamental facade, the concept is still Charleston single house in layout. It rises two floors above its basement, with stone steps and fancy wrought iron railings leading to a magnificent front door. A long, high wall surrounds a large,

tree-filled side garden with a cottage, which is overlooked by double piazzas and a side entrance.

The drawing room, library, and dining room have matching motifs. This mansion's interior is enchanting. Each ceiling is laden with elaborate molded plaster work in layers of Victorian eclectic romanticism.

The library or back sitting room. The house is filled with family heirlooms, art, china, silver, and furniture from Charleston, America, Europe, and the Orient.

The dining room contains rare Nanking and Canton china (ca. 1780) and French crystal chandelier and candle sticks. The drapes are of lined silk and wool made in 1929.

The bedroom dressed for summer, with white tester and cover on the four-poster bed, and no rug on a bare pine floor.

The Gibbes Museum of Art

135 Meeting Street

The Gibbes Museum of Art formally opened on April 11, 1905, with an exhibition of paintings. The building was designed by architect Frank Milburn, and the Rotunda is the gallery's centerpiece. Today the museum houses over five thousand works of largely American art. Exhibits include portraits of past notable figures, a Miniature Room with replicas of historic buildings, a collection of miniature portraits, and the Renaissance Gallery showcasing popular local artists of the 1920s and 1930s.

Map of Charleston